CRAIG

- T/M

Tim's Bon Mots

Witty Sayings and Good Quotes

for All Occasions

Tim Dunton, Editor

Tim's Bon Mots, Tim Dunton, Editor
4th Edition
Copyright © 2019 by Dunton Publishing

ISBN-13: 978-0692543191

Dunton Publishing
New York, New York
duntonpublishing.com

Introduction

Do you love witty sayings, but are disappointed by the lame stuff in books of quotations? If so, *Tim's Bon Mots* is for you. We've been collecting these for decades and have eliminated those that are too common, too corny, or just not clever enough.

The goal of this book is to become the repository of the kind of saying that you wish you could remember and have ready for just the right time.

Looking for the dirty or hateful ones? Insults not insulting enough for you? To shield tender minds, we have restricted that stuff to the e-book edition at amazon.com/ Tims-Bon-Mots-ebook. But please! Use Bon Mots for good, not for evil.

TABLE OF CONTENTS

LIFE

Despite the high cost of living, it remains popular.

By the time a man realizes his father was right, he has a son who thinks he's wrong.

Wisdom is knowing what to overlook.

Knowledge is knowing a tomato is a fruit. Wisdom is not putting it in a fruit salad.

Time is the best teacher, but it kills all its students.

Life is too short to be busy.

To be sure of hitting the target, shoot first and call whatever you hit the target.

Happiness is a good sense of humor and a bad memory.

The secret to life is knowing when to stop; leave the party while you're still wanted.

Karma means I can rest easily knowing all the people I treated badly had it coming.

I asked God for a bike, but I know God doesn't work that way. So I stole a bike and asked forgiveness.

It doesn't get any easier, you just get better at it.

It's ok to trade the possibility of your 80s and 90s for more guaranteed fun your 20s and 30s.

It's nice to be important, but it's more important to be nice.

It will be all right in the end. If it's not all right, it's not the end.

You don't solve your problems; you outgrow them.

Trying to understand reality in words is like trying to drink the ocean with a fork.

You can't talk yourself out of problems you behaved yourself into.

Happiness is having a large, loving, close-knit family in another city.

I'm not afraid of dying, I'm afraid of not living.

Luck bats last.

Moral is when you feel good afterward. Immoral is when you feel bad afterward.

Life is full of misery and suffering and is over much too soon.

You can do anything you want in life as long as you can find someone else to pay for it.

Winning isn't important as long as you win.

All it takes to get from nowhere to now here is to stop for a moment.

The grass is always greener on TV.

If you don't become the ocean, you will be seasick every day.

Who you are is the price you paid for what you wanted.

At the end of the game, the king and pawn both go into the same box.

It is not light at the end of the tunnel, it is a donut-shaped tube that has better lighting in some places than others.

In a fight between you and the world, bet on the world.

Life is a comedy for those who think and a tragedy for those who feel.

Life may have no meaning at all. Worse yet, it could have a meaning of which I disapprove.

The first half of life is ruined by your parents, the second by your kids.

Life may not be worth living, but what else can you do with it?

The future is much like the present, but considerably longer.

90% of success is just shutting up.

Bad decisions make good stories.

No longer needing an answer is as good as getting one.

Life is a sexually-transmitted terminal disease.

It may be lonely at the top, but it's a bitch at the bottom.

A pessimist sees the difficulty in every opportunity. An optimist sees the opportunity in every difficulty.

An optimist is someone who believes this is the best of all possible worlds. A pessimist is someone who fears the optimist is right.

If this is the best of all possible worlds, it is better that you don't know it.

An optimist is someone who is always looking for a new definition of the word optimist.

It's not who you know, it's who knows you.

Free will is the only choice.

The only thing you can really count on is your hand.

The difference between a rut and a grave is their depth.

Being wise is just being more aware of your faults and folly.

Better to be a coward for a minute than dead for the rest of your life.

Go ahead and feel bad if it makes you feel better.

Life

What other people think of me is none of my business.

I don't care what anyone thinks. What do you think about that?

It ain't over 'til it's not over.

When you die, your memories are not lost, they are shared with all who have lived before you.

If you're searching for something more, maybe you'll find it in less.

Success is becoming who you are, as much as possible.

We don't see things as they are; we see things as we are.

You don't get what you wish for; you get what you are.

The only true success is living life on your own terms.

I don't want to know what happens after death. I want it to be a surprise.

I'd gladly give up knowing the meaning of life for the experience of being fully alive.

Insanity – believing you need something you don't already have.

The danger is not that we aim too high and miss it, but that we aim too low and hit it.

You don't have to know where you're going to know you're going in the right direction.

Wherever you go, there you are.

You can have it all, just not all at once.

It's better not to have an extraordinary ability because then you might think you need to accomplish something great instead of simply enjoying life.

Seven days without working out makes one weak.

Nothing tastes as good as health feels.

It's not the size of the dog in the fight; it's the size of the fight in the dog.

A happy life is just a string of happy moments. But many people don't allow the happy moment because they're so concerned with trying to get a happy life.

You get what you settle for.

A closed mouth gathers no feet.

I'd rather be approximately right than precisely wrong.

It's better to be inconsistent than consistently wrong.

It's always darkest before it gets completely black.

The universal mistake – thinking that current trends will continue.

Brevity is the soul of lingerie.

Life

The greatest difficulty in communication is the illusion that it has been accomplished.

When communication is unsuccessful, it is the fault of the person trying to communicate.

That which does not kill me makes me stranger.

That which does not kill me makes me gain weight.

That which does not kill me didn't try hard enough.

Life's greatest burden is having nothing to carry.

The less things change, the more they remain the same.

Life is not fair. It's a good thing for you it isn't.

I don't expect life to be fair, but I would like it to be unfair in my favor.

The future isn't what it used to be.

The problem is not that we have problems. The problem is thinking that we shouldn't have problems.

The more you try to avoid pain, the more you will feel it when it comes.

The secret to predicting the future is to update frequently.

The best way to predict the future is to invent it.

Time is nature's way of keeping everything from happening at once.

Comfort doth make cowards of us all.

Perfection is the lowest standard of achievement. Doing is the highest.

Perfect means doing nothing wrong. Doing nothing wrong means doing nothing at all.

When a mouse laughs at a cat, there is usually a hole nearby.

The speed at which a man is running relates directly to what he is running from.

I need a serious re-shaking of the Etch-A-Sketch.

No one forgets where he buried the hatchet.

There are two ways to be happy; 1) get what you want, 2) want what you get.

Success is getting what you want. Happiness is wanting what you get.

The best things in life aren't things.

He who laughs, lasts.

Life is wasted on the living.

The best revenge is not needing any.

Reality is overrated.

Guessing is more fun than knowing.

Hard work pays off in the future. Laziness pays off now.

The mystery of life is not a problem to be solved, but a reality to be experienced.

Our desire is infinite, but our capacity for pleasure is not.

To err is human, but to really fuck things up you need a computer.

Is man God's best invention – or is God man's best invention?

The purpose of evolution is to invent God.

If we don't sin, Jesus died for nothing.

That which is understood does not need to be explained.

I'll forgive him after I kill him.

Those who do not remember the past are doomed to get Alzheimer's.

Those who ignore history are entitled to repeat it.

Those who do not learn from clichés are bound to repeat them.

You're as small as your controlling desires and as big as your dominant aspirations.

If you live each day to the fullest, you will probably stay up very late.

If you live each day as if it were your last, you would have very dirty underwear because who would want to wash clothes on the last day of his life?

Travel broadens; staying put deepens.

Life is simple. It's explaining it that is so difficult.

I embrace change because I never figured out what to do it the first place.

Simplicity is the ultimate sophistication.

You don't need to search for the nature of reality. Reality will find you soon enough.

Experience is the name we give to our mistakes.

Experience enables you to recognize a mistake when you make it again.

You make the bed. You do the dishes. And six months later you have to do to all over again.

Give a man food and he will eat for a day. Give a man a job and he will get 30 – 60 minutes to eat.

Give a man a fish and he will eat for a day. Teach him how to fish and he will sit in a boat and drink beer all day.

Build a man a fire and he will be warm for a day; light the man on fire and he will be warm for the rest of his life.

Give a man a job and he'll work all day. Teach a man to delegate and he'll take the rest of the day off.

Nothing is as good or as bad as it first seems.

A happy ending doesn't last forever.

It is only possible to live happily ever after on a day-to-day basis.

The size of your problems adjusts to fit your capacity to handle them.

The sooner we put it off, the more time we will have to do it.

The sooner you fall behind, the more time you will have to catch up.

If you wait until the last minute to do it, it will only take a minute to do.

Punctuality is the thief of time.

When you are having the peak experiences of your life, you do not recognize them as that. That is fortunate.

I'm less concerned with the eternity that will take place after I die than the eternity that I missed before I was born.

The unlived life is worth examining.

I don't wonder why things are how they are, I just wonder that they are how they are.

Some things in life can never be appreciated by a virgin.

You do some of your best living through those you leave behind.

The way to happiness is not to avoid unhappiness.

Life's a bitch. If it were a slut, it would be easy.

If I'm every on life support, unplug me. Then plug me in. See if that works.

All I know about life is that more is better.

Life is divided into thirds: youth, middle age, and "you look good."

The secret to happiness is low expectations.

Happiness is an optimistic nature, a love of beauty, and bad eyesight.

Happy people don't have the best of everything. They make the best of everything.

You may not be able to make your life longer, but you can make it deeper and wider.

Time is always money, but money is not always time. Therefore, time is worth more than money.

FLATTERY

Your body is the shine of the life force, the very flower of our species, a garden of earthly delights, a bounty that tests the limits of greed, an embarrassment of riches, proof that God loves us, a sight that would stir the blood of a dead man.

It makes the bravest heart beat faster.

God would not have created a body like yours if he didn't have a plan for me.

Have you been Photoshopped?

You are just the right amount of wrong.

Your magic is very powerful.

You wash up real nice.

Your breasts are all-powerful. What is thy bidding?

You're the same kind of different as me.

Your name is in every password I've ever had.

My heart has never smiled so hard.

I wish I could turn back the clock so I could have met you sooner and loved you longer.

You are both my greatest weakness and my greatest strength.

When I wake up, I'm going to come looking for you.

When I am near you, all my thoughts of birth control like smoke on a cloudy day.

When I am near you, I feel that evolution is compelling me forward. I owe it to my ancestors to pursue you.

When I look at you, I see God revealing himself.

Why do I like you so much?

The most effective means of flattery is telling people exactly what they think of themselves.

When I count my blessings, I count you twice.

How does it feel to be so good-looking?

I would drink your bathwater.

I started out painting the sunrise, but it ended up being you.

I want to think about the things you think about.

I like you just the way I am.

Flattery

You had me at boobs.

Yours is a beauty built in, not added on.

You are the best hormonal delusion I have ever had.

You vibrate at exactly my frequency.

You are so good-looking that Bigfoot would take your picture.

I wish my mother were alive so I could bring you home to her.

I learn new things about myself when I am with you.

The reflection in your eyes shows me the man I want to be.

I love looking into your eyes, but it's even better when you close them.

If I never see someone more beautiful than you, that will be just fine.

Every fantasy of my success includes the image of your admiration.

If I were a zombie, I'd eat you the most.

You are as appealing as the prospect of a beneficent God.

If you were the last piece of pizza on earth, I would lick you so that no one else would eat you.

When I first saw you, I realized I'd been frozen in a block of ice for years and was only starting to thaw.

You have accessed parts of me I never knew existed.

You reflect that light remarkably well.

You are difficult to look at. It is as if I will be struck down prematurely for taking in more beauty than I deserve.

The air in room where you are right now must be having its best day ever.

I bask in your grace.

I like my body when it is with your body.

I want to do with you what Spring does with the cherry trees.

Your aura has an aura.

I want to melt into you and live inside your skin.

The more clothes you take off, the better your body gets.

I would follow a trail of your shit just to see where it came from.

There are some things that cannot be put into words. For the first time, I am happy about that.

If you do not love me, the birds will have sung for nothing and the flowers will have bloomed in vain.

Flattery

You are the kind of woman a mirror likes to see.

Don't buy any more mirrors. The mirror should pay you.

You are a gravitational force against which I am powerless.

If God had a refrigerator, your picture would be on it.

I hope I die one day before you do so that I never know the world without you.

I hate to see you go, but I love to watch you leave.

I exist only to appreciate your beauty.

Your age sits lightly upon your wonderful shoulders.

To me you are both longing and the end of longing.

Are you real?

I view my life as two parts. One is before I met you and is in black and white. The other is after a met you and is in full color.

When I look at your picture on my computer, the cooling fan goes on, my contact lenses fog up, and my heart beat sets off the car alarm.

To get a face like that, you must have made a pact with the devil.

Do you think of a new way to be cute every day?

The best part about growing old is that I stay close to your age

If I could rearrange the alphabet, I'd put U and I together.

I have finally found something that matches my capacity for awe.

Your giggles are like champagne bubbles.

The first time I saw you, I melted into a pool of butter on the floor.

I would start a small country just so I could put your face on a postage stamp and lick the back of your head.

I want to die in your arms.

You are far more attractive than you need to be.

You do all the wrong things right.

I exist to buy you shoes.

I feel immortal when I am with you.

I regret that I have but two eyes to view you with.

From the time I first saw you I knew it was true -- you are my mating unit.

You are both my greatest strength and my greatest weakness.

Creation clearly favors you.

What gives you the right to be perfect?

When I see you I ache so strongly with desire that I feel my soul shudder.

His writing is so good that, when you read it, he is not on trial - you are.

It's not fair. God gave you too much.

You may be Satan, but you're my Satan.

Your presence in my life obligates me to maximize my life span.

I hold you in the light of God.

I have followed your beauty from the outside in. And I want to stay.

You're one of me and I'm one of you.

In your aura I experience the majesty of the cosmos.

From the moment I laid eyes on you, it was like I'd been reunited with someone I'd been madly in love with for hundreds of years.

I have abandoned my defenses. The flames are consuming me.

When I close my eyes, you're still there.

You've got to stop taking those ugly pills. They're just not working.

If I hadn't met you, I'd have a lot more money and I'd be out having fun every night. And I'd be looking for someone like you.

Your presence in my life obligates me to maximize my life span.

I hold you in the light of God

I have followed your beauty from the outside in. And I want to stay.

You're one of me and I'm one of you.

Honesty

Honesty is the best policy. Now what's the second best policy?

He can be counted on the do the right thing – after all other possibilities have been exhausted.

He's as crooked as a dog's hind leg.

He's as crooked as a barrel of fishhooks.

He who says he enjoys a cold shower in the morning will also lie about other things.

It was a poetic interpretation of the truth.

He's morally retarded.

He leads a rich fantasy life.

He cuts corners going up on two wheels.

He's following in his father's fingerprints.

Character is what you reveal when no one is watching.

He performed skillful surgery with the facts.

Two wrongs don't make a right, but three rights make a left.

He is economical with the truth.

He's been completely honest because he's never had a big enough opportunity.

He has what it takes to take what you have.

People will believe anything if you whisper it.

He makes a very good point, but it doesn't have the added advantage of being true.

He seldom encounters a fact he can't improve on.

I tried to be honest, but the truth got in the way.

He's indebted to his imagination for his facts.

He doesn't let the truth get in the way of a good story.

His love a good story outweighs his allegiance to the truth.

Truth was more of a stranger than fiction.

He considers the redistribution of wealth to be a personal responsibility.

I see his hands are in his own pocket for a change.

He's a member of the impressionist school of truth.

Honesty

He pursues his relationship with the truth through extensive use of artistic license.

He's robbing Peter to rob Paul.

His opinion is unburdened by facts.

How are you?

Not very horrible.

I can sit up and take nourishment.

Another day closer to death.

All vital signs within normal limits.

Better than I need to be.

Much better.

It may look like I'm doing nothing, but at the cellular level I'm actually quite busy.

Sick, sober, and sorry.

I need a good cry.

Other than my overwhelming sense of impending doom, I'm fine thanks.

All physical needs have been met.

I'm lost, but I'm making really good time.

I'm stronger at the broken places.

They say I'm very good.

I feel very pretty today.

Cold, wet, and happy.

If I weren't so happy, I'd be miserable.

Better than I look.

Overpaid, underworked.

I've got a stomach full of empty.

Falling apart at the expected rate.

I'm alright, it's everyone else I'm worried about.

I am wallowing in self-pity.

I'm much happier now that I've stopped trying to get in the shortest line.

Feeling single, seeing double.

Happier than a bird with a french fry.

Happier than a camel on Wednesday.

Still on the right side of the grass.

I think I'm good, I don't know what other people think.

Very merry.

How Are You?

Infected, inflamed, and infuriated.

Too dumb for New York, too ugly for L.A.

I think I'm in love.

Same shit, different day.

Aces.

Fine, as long as I don't think about it too much.

Good and getting better.

Better than I deserve.

Better than yesterday, not as good as tomorrow.

Partying like a rock star.

I need a little time off for bad behavior.

Livin' the dream.

Livin' large and stickin' it to the man.

Just about right.

Right as rain, mate.

Fat and happy.

No outstanding warrants, no known terminal diseases.

There's no permanent damage.

Nobody's complaining.

Too beautiful to die. Too wild to live.

All is proceeding according to plan.

All is at it should be.

I'm just the way I look.

Absolutely, positively, not guilty.

Waves of well-being are washing over me.

I'm glad that things can be so bad and yet I'm still happy.

How's it Going?

Very quickly.

Straight and narrow.

Well indeed.

Living in accordance with my genetic destiny.

Living off the kindness of strangers.

If you knew how well I was doing, you'd probably hate me.

I don't know, but I hope it doesn't stop.

I am living so well that death will tremble to take me.

Politics

Democracy is four wolves and a lamb deciding what to have for dinner.

The best argument against democracy is a conversation with the average voter.

Democratic is the name we give to people when we need them.

I'd rather die on my feet than live on my knees.

Power corrupts the few; weakness corrupts the many.

Knowledge is power. Power corrupts. So study hard and be evil.

Knowledge is not power. Action is power. Knowledge without action is useless.

A fine is a tax for doing wrong. A tax is a fine for doing well.

He's a red meat, rock-ribbed Ronald Reagan Republican.

Nobody gives you power, you have to take it.

He's tolerant of everything except people who disagree with him.

Recession: when your neighbor loses his job. Depression: when you lose your job. Recovery: when Barack Obama loses his job.

Crime means you take the money and run. Politics means you run and then take the money.

It's not the have and have-nots; it's the wills and will-nots.

When threatened with a gun, you will have the rest of your life to think through your position on gun control.

90% of politicians give the other 10% a bad name.

A diplomat is someone who tells you to go to hell in such a way that you look forward to the trip.

The worst inequality is to make unequal things equal.

Free people are not equal and equal people are not free.

The bigger the government, the smaller the citizen.

From each according to his ability, to each according to his contribution.

Hitler was a anti-smoking, vegetarian and animal-rights activist who thought in terms of race, class, and gender.

War does not determine who is right – only who is left.

The upper crust is a bunch of crumbs held together by dough.

For every action there is an equal and opposite government program.

All men are created equally prejudiced.

A liberal is someone who feels a great debt to society and wants you to pay it.

Someone who robs Peter to pay Paul can always count on the support of Paul.

Grab them by their balls and their hearts will follow.

All it takes for evil to flourish is for good men to do nothing.

The land of bilk and money.

The land of the free gift with purchase.

Old soldiers never die – just the young ones.

A government big enough to give you everything is a government big enough to take everything away.

It's not who casts the votes, it's who counts them.

In capitalism, resources are unequally distributed. In socialism, everyone is equally miserable.

He's a thumb-sucking, bedwetting, weak-kneed, left handed, limp-wristed, lily-livered, low testosterone, hemophiliac liberal.

Conservatives divide the world into good and evil. Liberals divide the world between rich and poor.

Whether you are a conservative or liberal depends on whether you are more scared of big government or big corporations.

He's grabbing at more straws than Michael Moore at a milkshake factory.

If you lie to the government, it's a felony. If they lie to you, it's politics.

A liberal is a humanist who hasn't been mugged yet.

Poverty does not have causes. Wealth has causes.

He shrinks his world to fit his world view.

Rules to Live By

Live every day as if it were your first.

Think about how happy you would be if you lost everything you have and then suddenly got it back.

The most effective way to live in the moment and focus on the here and now is to engage in sexual activity.

God grant me the serenity to change the things I can't accept; the courage to blame everyone else; and the wisdom to know the difference.

God grant me the serenity to change the people I can change; injure those I can't; and the wisdom to hide the evidence.

If you drive, don't park. Accidents cause people.

If at first you don't succeed, read the directions.

If at first you don't succeed, skydiving is not for you.

If at first you don't succeed, redefine success.

If at first you do succeed, try something harder.

When all else fails, lower your expectations.

Platinum Rule: Do unto others as they would want done unto them.

Before enlightenment, chop wood, carry water. After enlightenment, chop wood, carry water.

First secure an independent income. Then practice virtue.

There's a deception to every rule.

When it's your turn to die, sing your death song, let the world embrace you, and die like you're going home.

Be moderate in all things, including moderation.

The best way to destroy your enemies is to make friends with them.

Instead of trying to love your enemies, be nicer to your friends.

If you assume a certain number of people won't like you no matter what you do, you will prevent that same number of worries.

Don't look at where you fell. Look at where you slipped.

Don't worry about keeping your heart healthy. It will last as long as you live.

When tempted to fight fire with fire, remember that the fire department usually uses water.

Rules to Live By

When your horse is dead, get off it.

As long as you belittle, you will be little.

Keep your friends close, but your envious closer.

Seek first to understand, then to be understood.

If a thing is worth doing, it would have been done already.

If you want others to be happy, practice compassion. If you want to be happy, practice compassion.

Be a good person now so they don't have to lie about you at your funeral.

Be the person your dog thinks you are.

Cultivate selective ignorance.

Praise by name; criticize by category.

Don't try to walk across a river just because it has an average depth of three feet.

When you have a choice to be right or kind, be kind.

If you can't be kind, at least be vague.

Don't try to keep up with the Joneses; drag them down to your level.

Don't believe everything you think.

Trivialize the trivial.

To understand all is to forgive all, but you can't understand. all, so don't expect to forgive all.

Dress for the weather you want, not the weather you have. If you want to be somebody, be yourself.

Instead of trying to be better than others, be more like yourself than they can be.

Never ascribe to malice what can be explained by incompetence.

Be the kind of person you'd like to meet.

Do things in chronological order; it's less confusing that way.

Make the present good and the past will take care of itself.

Don't be so focused on what you're looking for that you overlook what you find.

Be strong enough to to have enemies.

Imagine your death. Now do what would make it ok.

If you can't stand the heat, get out and start bitchin'.

You can't get any smarter or better looking, so you might as well try to be nicer.

Be suspicious of anyone who has a strong opinion on a complicated issue.

When you were born, you cried and the world rejoiced.

Live so that when you die, the world will cry and you will rejoice.

Strive not have the best of everything, but to make the best of everything.

Before criticizing someone, walk a mile in their shoes. That way, when you criticize them, you're a mile away and you have their shoes.

Don't give back; give forward.

Trust Allah and tie up your camel.

Do for yourself what you could have others do for you.

Be careful what you wish for. Your enemy might get it.

Empty what's full; fill what's empty.

First do what you need to, then do what you can.

Rules are for the obedience of fools and cowards and for the guidance of the wise and brave.

If you find it difficult to embrace change, just accept uncertainty and let the change take care of itself.

Don't trust a person who doesn't like dogs, but do trust a dog who doesn't like a person.

Dance like non one is watching. Email like it will be read aloud in a deposition.

If you want to be one with everything, you have to have one of everything.

It is like spelling "banana." You have to know when to stop.

If you are going to commit a crime, do it with someone more important than you. That way, if you are caught, the prosecutor will offer a deal to testify against the other guy, but he won't give the other guy a deal to testify against you.

Help a man when he is trouble and he will remember you when he is in trouble again.

You will catch more flies with manure than honey or vinegar.

Proceed with the confidence of a burgeoning universe.

WORK

Monday is the root of all evil.

Whatever hits the fan won't be evenly distributed.

Be nice to the people you meet on the way up because they are the same people you will meet on the way down.

A bus station is where a bus stops. A train station is where a train stops. I work at a work station.

The harder you work, the harder it is to surrender.

Hard work never killed anyone supervising it.

Hard work never killed anyone, but why take the chance?

The cemetery is full of indispensable men.

No man is truly successful until his mother-in-law admits it.

She became a medium because anything of hers well done was rare.

I always arrive for work late, but I make up for it by leaving early.

If I had known I was going to do so well, I would have tried harder.

If I had known what it would be like to have it all, I might have been willing to settle for less.

Most people get paid just enough for them not to quit and work just hard enough not to get fired.

To make a long story short, there's nothing like the boss walking in.

He climbed the ladder of success kissing the feet of the guy above him and kicking the head of the guy below him.

He climbed the ladder of success wrong by wrong.

It's not whether you win or lose; it's how you place the blame.

It's not whether you win or lose; it's whether I win or lose.

He's not lazy; he has an infinite capacity for leisure.

He's not lazy. He's a relaxaholic.

He's not lazy. He just rests before he gets tired.

He's not lazy, he just really enjoys doing nothing.

He's not lazy, he's an expert at maximizing his free time.

He's not lazy, he just started at the bottom and liked it there.

He's not lazy, he's physically conservative.

He's not lazy, he's just time-affluent.

He faces his problems one tomorrow at a time.

He thinks he's practicing Christianity when he loafs and fishes.

He went beyond the call of duty to get even further away from it.

He's going through the revolving door of life on someone else's push.

He's taking a "wait and see" attitude about his life. He's living on "Someday Isle."

There are seven days in a week. He thinks someday is one of them.

I wasn't sleeping, I was looking at the inside of my eyelids.

He's trying to sleep his way to the middle.

His life's ambition is to be a fart ventriloquist.

If you want to quit your job to spend more time with your family, check with your family first.

The A students teach the B students. The B students work for the C students.

The best way to look good to your boss is to make him look good to his boss.

You've got to work hard to get good enough to get into a position to get lucky.

I want to be the first person to have his last words be: "I wish I spent more time at the office."

He's good at multi-tasking. He can waste time, be unproductive, and procrastinate all at once.

The first five days after the weekend are the hardest.

They pay me just enough to keep me from quitting and I work just hard enough to keep from getting fired.

He's on eternity leave.

The first five days after the weekend are the hardest.

What Are You?

I am a twinkling of electrical charges inside a sack of bio-chemicals.

I am an aperture through which the universe is observing itself.

I am a DNA-replicating machine specializing in the stimulation and satisfaction of appetites.

I am either a host to God or hostage to ego.

I am a speck of awareness on a wing of a butterfly, among a pulsing swarm of butterflies.

I am not a drop in the ocean, I am the entire ocean in a drop.

I am a flowering of universal consciousness.

I am not a human being having a spiritual experience. I am a spiritual being having a human experience.

I am a randomly-mutating germ giving multiple aphorisms.

I am an ego floating in a bag of skin.

I am a meat suit with memories.

I am molecules that rearrange food.

I am nothing but a bundle of perceptions, but that's good enough for me.

I am life support for my sexual organs.

BAD PLACE

It is so cold there that the flashers have to give verbal descriptions.

It is so cold there that they have to chip dogs off of fire hydrants.

Many were cold; few were frozen.

It's a wretched hive of scum and villainy.

The town does not give up her charms easily.

The town is so dull, the female impersonators are women.

The town is so dull, the prostitutes are virgins.

The town is so dull that the tide went out and wouldn't come back.

It was so windy, you could spit in your own eye.

It was wetter than a reunion of the lesbian swim team.

I am nothing but a bundle of perceptions, but that's good enough for me.

I am life support for my sexual organs.

Bad Time

It's good and it's original, but the parts that are good aren't original and the parts that are original aren't good.

It wasn't just original, it was aboriginal.

The covers of the book are too far apart.

It finished too long after the end.

It gives bullshit a bad name.

It wasn't as bad as the thought of it.

Give me librium or give me meth.

It was the opposite of sex. It was bad even when it was good.

The conductor didn't know his brass from his oboe.

The band should be forced to disband due to excessive sax and violins.

The play was a success, but the audience was a disaster.

It was all retch and no vomit.

It was like taking the SATs while cheerleading tryouts are taking place outside the open window.

There's more bullshit in that than in the Fort Worth stockyards.

It is difficult to forget, but well worth the effort.

The topic kept coming up like a bad meal.

It was like a woman's breasts – infinitely fascinating, yet ultimately unsatisfying.

I shaved my balls for this?

I've seen better film in my shower.

That was bad on bad.

That's deader than disco.

It was the bland leading the bland.

It was cornier than Kansas in July.

It was so syrupy, I felt like eating waffles.

It was just realistic enough to make you care how un-realistic it was.

When something is too stupid to be spoken, it is sung.

That was the worst thing I never wanted to hear.

Bad Time

It's been real and it's been fun, but it hasn't been real fun.

I sat through the whole thing and I feel older because of it.

It was ok, but it's just not my stack of porn.

It was 10 lbs of shit in a 5 lb. bag.

That's the kind of dirty that won't wash off.

That was time well wasted. Let's call it a nightmare.

It had more twists and turns than a plate of spaghetti.

It read like it was translated into Chinese and back into English.

Someone threw a turd into the punch bowl.

Thanks, but throw the rest down the toilet and cut out the middleman.

It's best eaten when very hungry.

It works well in practice, but it will never work in theory.

I went there for a nice meal, but ended up just reloading my shit gun.

It feels so good when it stops.

How could a just God allow such a performance?

It was better than submersing your head in an unflushed toilet.

It was better than having your skin ripped off with a pair of plyers.

He should take two weeks off. And then quit.

I thought it was going to be a horror movie, but it turned out it was just a horrible movie.

It was somewhat better than a stinking pile of excrement on a hot summer day.

DRINK

Vacation in a bottle.

I have a drinking problem - no money!

I killed a 6-pack just to watch it die.

If you can't be with the wine you love, love the wine you're with.

Beer got me into this mess, and, with God as my witness, beer is going to get me out.

24 hours in a day. 24 beers in a case. Coincidence?
I think not.

No taxation without intoxication.

He got his degree in relaxation therapy from Ale University.

Drink up and be somebody!

Drunkenness: temporary suicide.

The high cost of living is nothing like the cost of living high.

The days of wine and neurosis.

Thirst things first.

I went into the bar optimistically and I left misty optically.

Alcohol creates more people than it kills.

There is no situation so bad that a few drinks won't make it worse.

I'm sadder, Budweiser.

I may be an alcoholic, but you are an assoholic.

Not to get technical, but, chemically speaking, alcohol actually is a solution.

You can't buy happiness, but you can buy beer.

Instead of warning pregnant women not to drink, they should tell drunk women not to have sex.

It takes only one drink to get me drunk. The problem is I can't remember whether it's the 13th or 14th.

Alcohol – the universal lubricant.

He's leading a liquid lifestyle.

He's such an alcoholic that when pink elephants get drunk, they see him.

I know more old drunks than old doctors.

When I read about the dangers of drinking, I gave up reading.

Drink

I drink you to sleep every night.

After the third beer, the beer is drinking the man.

I was forced to survive for a week on nothing but food and water.

Alcohol never solves problems, but, then again, neither does milk.

He was so drunk, he had to hug the grass to keep from falling off the earth.

He was adrift on the ether of alcohol.

If you drink like a fish, swim, don't drive.

I got so drunk that I fell down and missed the floor.

I've been sober for 17 days, but they haven't been all in a row.

Love makes the world go round, but whiskey makes it go around twice as fast.

I used to drink, but that was hours ago.

I don't have a problem with alcohol, I have a problem without alcohol.

I'm not a social drinker, it's more work-related.

I come from a long line of alcoholics. My family tree has a car wrapped around it.

There are more important things in life than alcohol, but alcohol makes up for not having them.

I always take things with a grain of salt. Plus a slice of lemon, and a shot of tequila.

I've never had more than one drink at a time.

A good servant, but a bad master.

Grip it, tip it, sip it.

If life deals you lemons, make a pitcher of whiskey sours.

A weekend wasted in not a wasted weekend.

Wine hangover – The Wrath of Grapes.

The best way to avoid a hangover is to start drinking early.

He who hoots with the owls at night will not soar with the eagles at dawn.

I drink to make other people more interesting.

The hand that sells the whisky controls the tomahawk.

Partying is such sweet sorrow.

I've been drinking about my thinking problem.

He has a big hole in his face where his beer should be.

Beauty is in the eye of the beerholder.

Drink

I don't need glasses; I drink straight from the bottle.

Champagne for my friends; real pain for my sham friends.

Religions change. Beer remains.

Think globally; drink locally.

I spent 90% of my money on booze. The rest I wasted.

He's not homeless, he's an urban outdoorsman in the wine business.

He's not panhandling. He's kick starting an alternative lifestyle campaign.

I have brain cells that will remember tonight. I want them destroyed.

Everyone needs to believe in something. I believe I'll have another beer.

I'd rather have a bottle in front of me than a frontal lobotomy.

I haven't touched a drop of alcohol since the invention of the funnel.

You ain't much fun since I quit drinking.

I thought you asked "Do you want some tequila," not "do you want something to kill ya."

One tequila, two tequila, three tequila, floor.

In dog beers, I've had only one.

They say I have a drinking problem, but I don't have a problem drinking at all.

When you're done drinking, stop drinking.

He gave in to beer pressure.

He's looking at life through the bottom of a glass.

I now know that I don't have to have fun in order to drink alcohol.

It takes about thirty years of drinking for booze to kill you. My life expectancy is 85 years old. So I'm going to start drinking heavily at 55 and the booze will never kill me.

If you add alcohol to worms in a laboratory jar, it will kill them. So if you have worms, drink alcohol.

That's what happens when you drink on an empty head.

The first time he played Spin the Bottle, he just wanted to drink from it.

PEOPLE

The only normal people are those who you don't know well.

A smart man knows everything; a shrewd man knows everyone.

Perfection is overrated.

The 11th commandment: Don't get caught.

He who lives by the sword dies by the gun.

The only common denominator in all your bad relationships is you.

All who wander are not lost.

That's not a woman, it's an estrogen-American.

The best way to get someone to stop talking is tell them they look sexy with their lips together.

I'll admit I was wrong as soon as I run out of people to blame.

The best way to find out if you can trust someone is to trust them.

The worst thing about getting to know people well is finding out how unhappy they are.

People don't care how much you know until they know how much you care.

He who is best at manipulating symbols is at highest risk of missing the underlying realities.

He's so macho that he castrates bulls with his teeth.

The fewer the facts, the stronger the opinion.

The worst snobs are those who recently rose just above the lowest levels.

I hope his consequences catch up with his actions before his actions catch up with my circumstances.

If you're bored, you're boring.

It's better to be looked over than overlooked.

I'm not great enough to be humble.

Happy people don't have to be fun.

If you laid all the healthy people end to end around the world, 67% of them would drown.

People just want to be listened to, understood, and appreciated. They also like to have their genitals licked.

When a man's best friend is his dog, that dog has a problem.

Only mediocre people are always at their best.

He's so boring that people throw parties just to not invite him.

Just because I don't care doesn't mean I don't understand.

If you think there's good in everybody, you haven't met everybody.

Anyone who goes to a psychiatrist ought to have his head examined.

If you didn't want to feel inferior to your classmates, you shouldn't have gone to such a good school.

I used to feel I was a woman trapped in a man's body. Then I was born.

He has so many good qualities that it's difficult to like him.

There's a fine line between fishing and standing on the shore like an idiot.

We may not have it all together, but together we have it all.

Hospitality is making your guests feel at home even when you wish they were.

Saints need sinners.

A woman is a baby's way of making another baby.

They go together like death and dismemberment.

They go together like feces and urine.

I don't care what anyone says about me, as long as it's not true.

Patience is what you have when there are too many witnesses.

In New York City, you can be a one in a million and there will be seven others exactly like you.

Negotiation is the art of letting someone else have your way.

The most unlovable people are the ones who need love the most.

Everybody's friend is nobody's friend.

Cream rises to the top. But so does scum.

You can judge a man's strength by the strength of his enemies.

People who think they know everything are particularly annoying to those of us who do.

If there really were someone who knew it all, you wouldn't know it because that person would know that people don't like know-it-alls so that he would keep quiet.

The only one more foolish than the guy who talks like he knows everything is the guy who argues with him.

You're just jealous because the voices talk only to me.

Holding a grudge is like taking poison to kill your enemy.

Wise men talk because they have something to say. Fools talk because they have to say something.

One who talks to you about others is a gossip. One who talks to you about himself is a bore. One who talks to you about yourself is a brilliant conversationalist.

A gentleman is someone who can play the accordion, and doesn't.

Trying to know yourself is like trying to bite your teeth.

When you're good with a hammer, everything looks like a nail.

A friend – someone who knows all about you and likes you anyway.

A friend – someone who, when asked how he is, tells you.

Friends are God's way of apologizing for your relatives.

Friends may come and go, but enemies accumulate.

Those who matter don't mind. Those who mind, don't matter.

Many a bark has been to avoid being bitten.

If you think you can live without others, you'll need to.

The more arguments you win, the fewer friends you will have.

Behind every generous person is another generous person.

A heart in the right place is easily moved.

We teach people how to treat us.

There are two kinds of people – those who believe the world can be divided into two kinds of people and those who don't.

There are three kinds of people – those who are good at math and those who aren't.

I'm into fitness. Fit'n this taco into my mouth.

He who signs the checks tells the funniest jokes.

It's ok to be stupid. And it's ok to be arrogant. But it's not ok to be stupid and arrogant.

If we didn't have shortcomings, we wouldn't enjoy it so much when we notice the shortcomings of others.

Whenever we think of people as animals, we become smarter. Whenever we think of animals as people, we become dumber.

Opinions are like assholes – not expressed too loudly.

Envy is the only one of the seven deadly sins that isn't any fun.

The best quality you can have is the ability to accurately observe your own processes.

If you're consistently unhappy with other people's behavior, you have done a poor job of forming your expectations.

When women hold off on marrying men, it's called independence. When men hold off on marrying women, it's called fear of commitment.

He's not a businessman. He's a business, man.

It helps to think you are better looking than you actually are. And it's good to think you are smarter than you actually are. But it's not good to think you are more important than you actually are.

Men want to risk their lives to be heroes while women do not. Both accept this because they consider only men to be disposable.

Happy people don't have the best of everything. They make the best of everything.

It's easy to solve other people's problems. It's hard to solve your own.

Logic is for people who can't feel correctly.

Age

How Old Are You?

Old enough to know better; too young to care.

Old enough to know how foolish I've been. Young enough to think I can change.

My death has saddled his horse and is heading my way.

Too young for Medicare; too old for men to care.

Too old to be a rising star; too young to be one of a dying breed.

I am as old as yesterday and young as tomorrow.

I am as old as eternity and as young as the sunrise. My age is none of my business.

I am older than dirt, but I can still get dirty.

I am older than I've even been before.

I've been around the sun 40 times.

I am older than spring, but younger than winter.

Not including weekends, I'm 39.

I'm 39 with 25 years of experience.

He who dies last, gets the most toys.

Middle age is when it takes longer to rest than to get tired.

Middle age is when broadness of the mind and narrowness of the waist change places.

I'm going to get old or die trying.

The worst part about outliving your acquaintances is that you can't tell them "I told you so" about their bad habits.

We spend the first half of our lives wishing we looked like someone else and the second wishing we looked like we used to.

The best thing about being 60 is that I can now say I'm a sextagenarian.

Father Time has caught up with Mother Nature.

Birthdays are good for you. Statistics show that people who have the most of them live the longest.

Life is like a roll of toilet paper. The closer you get to the end, the faster it goes.

When I was young, I wanted a BMW. Now I don't care about the W.

You don't stop exercising because you get old, you get old because you stop exercising.

He's younger than his eyes.

When I was a boy of fourteen, my father was so ignorant I could hardly stand to have the old man around. But when I got to be twenty-one, I was amazed by how much the old man had learned in just seven years.

The best way to get over the fear of old age is to get a cancer diagnosis.

About the time you learn to get the most out of life, most of it is gone.

Most people prefer the old days. They were younger then.

The older you get, the more foolish acts you have committed, but the less it bothers you.

Time is a great healer, but a bad beautician.

Old is when you have all the answers, but no one asks you the questions.

Older people are wiser because they know how much their own attitudes have changed.

When you are young, you want to change the world. When you are old, you want to change the young.

Old people love giving advice because it consoles them for no longer being capable of setting a bad example.

Only the young die good.

She said she's approaching 40, but she didn't say from what direction.

No wise man ever wished to be younger.

I hear the beating of the wings of the angel of death.

All of those "once in a lifetime" events are starting to add up!

You're only young once, but you can be immature forever.

Beautiful young people are works of nature. Beautiful old people are works of art.

Old age is the revenge of the ugly.

At my age, flowers scare me.

As you get older, the pickings get slimmer, but the people don't.

I can still jump as high as ever. I just can't stay up as long.

After you're over the hill, you pick up speed.

Being over the hill is better than being under it.

Remember a woman's birthday, but not her age.

Old is when you think more about what you did than what you're going to do.

You aren't old until your regrets replace your dreams.

Maturity is the ability to tolerate uncertainty.

Maturity is the ease with which we compromise.

Maturity – the ease with which we accept our limitations.

Maturing isn't about finding yourself. It is about creating yourself.

When I was young and stupid, I was young and stupid.

Age gets better with wine.

Age and treachery always win over youth and ambition.

People don't grow old. When they stop growing, they become old.

Wisdom doesn't always come with age. Sometimes age just shows up all by itself.

Old is when the candles cost more than the cake.

Forty is the old age of youth; fifty is the youth of old age.

At fifty, everyone has the face he deserves.

You will either invest your time and money in your health or spend them on your diseases. The only way to escape this fact is to die early.

You're only as old as the things you feel.

Old age is a high price to pay for maturity.

Time wounds all heals.

Maturity sounds good only to those who have recently attained it.

The best way to look younger is to hang around with older people.

The older I get, the better I was.

There are three stages of a man's life: 1) He believes in Santa Claus. 2) He doesn't believe in Santa Claus 3) He is Santa Claus.

There are three stages of a man's life: 1) He cares what people think of him 2) He doesn't care what people think of him. 3) He realizes no one's thinking about him.

There are seven stages of a man's life: spills, drills, thrills, bills, ills, pills, and wills.

Old people know more about being young than young people know about being old.

I'm not young enough to know everything.

Age

With age, beauty folds inward.

What she lacks in maturity, she makes up for in youth.

My goal is to die young, as late as possible.

I'm not old; I'm chronologically-gifted.

A good thing about getting old is that you can resist change without as many negative consequences.

The best thing about the good old days is that I wasn't good and I wasn't old.

The best thing about getting old is that a life sentence doesn't sound as bad as it used to.

When you're 87, you can do whatever your kids want you to.

I thought getting old would take longer

He's so old they have discontinued his blood type.

He's growing old disgracefully.

No one will ever say I was cut down too early.

I've made the shift from trying to better my situation to just enjoying it.

I thought getting old would take longer.

The best part of being old is finally realizing that your life is really not that important after all.

I thought getting old would take longer.

Love & Sex

Sex relieves tension; love causes it.

Better to copulate than never.

Sex is better than logic. Would you like me to prove it to you?

Sex doesn't take place between the legs; it takes place between the ears.

A man chases a woman until she catches him.

Sex is not just about sex.

Everything is about sex. Except sex. Sex is about power.

My wife and I do it doggie style. I sit up and beg. She rolls over and plays dead.

You won't hate yourself in the morning if we sleep until noon.
Lust is the sincerest form of attraction.

He is a cunning linguist.

He has restless genitals syndrome.

Stalking is the sincerest form of flattery.

It's better to be alone for the right reason than with someone for the wrong reason.

I thought sex was a pain in the ass. Then I turned over.

When a man complains that a woman has no heart, it's pretty certain that she has his.

The difference between friendship and love is how much you can hurt each other.

Love is all fun and games until someone loses an eye or gets pregnant.

It's usually a good idea to have sex with women. The mistake is in trying to possess them.

He has replaced sex with food. Now he can't even get into his own pants.

In ancient times, men sacrificed virgins to the gods. They were careful not to sacrifice sluts.

I want to sink into her arms without also falling into her hands.

He was as horny as bull moose during the rut.

Prostitution: the world's oldest purchase decision.

If you don't want to see me anymore, why do you keep showing up in my dreams every night?

If you can't live without me, why aren't you dead yet?

Your maidenhood is worth keeping, but worth more given up.

I don't think it could get any better, but let's keep trying.

We are a fastidious couple. She's fast and I'm hideous.

Incompatibility can work if the man has income and the woman is pattable.

Women will never be equal to men until they can walk down the street with a bald head and a beer gut and still think they are sexy.

It only hurts me when I cry.

Behind every successful man is a woman. Behind the fall of successful men is usually another woman.

Swapping spit, playing tonsil hockey, just putting one tongue in front of the other.

Tickling her fancy, slapping bellies, getting busy, getting sticky, getting straightened out, bumping uglies, mixing it up, getting tangled up, tickling and pickling, splitting the difference, sharing intimacies, re-enacting the primal scene, doing the horizontal hula, doing the dance of cre-ation, exchanging genetic material, making the two-backed beast, thrashing about, making ends meet, mattress danc-ing, downtime, putting the wig on Oscar, playing Hide the

Salami, planting the pole in peach pie, banging beaver, fogging up the windows, playing Doctors Without Borders, doing the wild thing, sparking, couch surfing, charming the snake, balancing their energy, sharing intimacies, joining at the hip, playing mommy and daddy, treating their restless genitals syndrome, expressing their creative processes, pole dancing, partnering, lowering themselves to each others' levels, doing what grownups do, spending quality time together, working the mattress.

Enjoying himself, choking his chicken, flogging his dolphin, yanking his crank, tending his wedding tackle, manipulating his meat pole, slamming his ham, tooting his own horn, dating himself, holding his own, wetting his whistle, beating his meat, keeping his tool sharp, palpitating his pal, making a man of himself, doing his own thing.

Bearded clam, the vertical smile, where the twain meet.

Brownholer, cornholer, fudgepacker.

Women should be obscene and not heard.

My fantasy is having two men at once – one cooking, one cleaning.

She's an orgasm waiting to happen.

Chaste makes waste.

It was an exercise in fertility.

Love & Sex

I wouldn't mind being the last man on earth just to see if all those women were telling me the truth.

Last night the sex was so good that even my neighbors had to have a cigarette afterward.

How can I miss you if you don't leave?

I like a woman with a head on her shoulders. I hate necks.

Women are not meant to be understood. They are meant to be loved.

Women need to decide whether a man is too old to be considered eligible or too eligible to be considered old.

I have sex almost every day – almost on Monday, almost on Tuesday...

Nothing takes the taste out of peanut butter like unrequited love.

The best cure for an unrequited loved is to get to know them better.

A lady is a woman who makes a man act like a gentleman.

The problem is that God gave man a brain and a penis, but only enough blood to run one of them at a time.

He is so hostile toward women, he sneaks into women's restrooms and puts the toilet seats up.

If I had to do it all over again, I'd do it all over you.

The last thing I want to do is hurt you. But it's still on my list.

I need a furry place to keep my nose warm.

Strip 'em, grip 'em, stroke 'em, poke 'em, bone 'em and own 'em.

One swallow does not a girlfriend make.

One in the bush is worth two in the hand.

I want to kiss you with every lip on my face.

Mustache riding.

Some are born to greatness. Some achieve greatness. Some have it thrust into them.

I wasn't kissing him, I was smelling his mustache.

I wasn't kissing her, I was whispering into her mouth.

There was a woman knocking on my door last night. Someone finally let her out.

It was boy meets girl; girl gets boy into pickle; boy gets pickle into girl.

Abstinence makes the heart grow fonder.

Absence makes the heart go wander.

What price getting laid if a man loses his manhood?

Necessity is the mother of attraction.

Not being able to have sex with all the women in the world is not a reason not to try.

Outside every thin woman is a fat man trying to get in.

She's not easy, she's horizontally-accessible.

She speaks five languages and can't say no in any of them.

Want to come over and look at my ceiling?

I can part my hair with my tongue.

I can play the *William Tell Overture* on my cell phone with my tongue.

My penis is made of chocolate and spouts money.

In the game of love, it's not whether you win or lose, it's whether you score.

They were playing hockey without a goalie.

It was a comedy of Eros.

It's not how deep you fish, it's how you wiggle your worm.

I have a firm rule about pursuing women. If they are firm, I pursue them.

I deal with women on the honor system. Get on her and stay on her.

Did you slide her the pink steel? Pack her pipe? Slide her the high hard one?

Did she close the deal with Mr. Johnson?

She greeted John Peter eye-to-eye.

I felt like a priapic satyr in a field of willing maidens.

She violated my standards faster than I could lower them.

Women like a strong silent man because they think he is listening to them.

They achieved multiple sarcasms.

She's so pure, even Moses couldn't part her knees.

The love that lasts the longest is that which is never returned.

An intellectual is someone who has found something more interesting than sex.

I will always love the false image I had of you.

Tell her I've been too fucking busy. Or vice versa.

Sex is a misdemeanor. The more you miss it, the meaner you get.

She can suck a golf ball through a garden hose, suck the chrome off a bumper hitch, suck-start a Harley.

A woman begins by resisting a man's advances and ends by blocking his retreat.

Men talk to women so they can sleep with them. Women sleep with men so they can talk to them.

A man is as good as he has to be and a woman is as bad as she dares.

A woman never forgets the men she could have had; a man never forgets the women he couldn't have.

Men mistake friendship, but not sex, for love; women mistake sex, but not friendship, for love.

To be happy with a man you must understand him a lot and love him a little. To be happy with a woman you must love her a lot and don't try to understand her at all.

Women need to feel love in order to have sex. Men need to have sex in order to feel love.

Women want one man for everything; men want every woman for one thing.

Women hope they can change a man. Men hope a woman won't change. Both are disappointed.

Men don't know how to say goodbye. Women don't know when to say it.

Women can fake an orgasm, but men can fake an entire relationship.

A man falls in love through his eyes, a woman through her ears.

Men will sleep with women they won't date. Women will date men they won't sleep with.

Men forget, but never forgive. Women forgive, but never forget.

Women are sex objects because men have evolved to desire the appearance of a woman's ability to care for children inside her body. Men are success objects because women have evolved to desire the appearance of a man's ability to care for children outside her body.

You don't really know a woman until you marry her. You don't really know a man until you work with him.

We have a love/hate relationship. We both love me and hate her.

When a woman has tears in her eyes, it's the man who cannot see.

I'm not a sex addict. I'm a polyamorous pleasure provider.

What is your pleasure threshold?

He wrote a bon mot to show that he loves her, but he wrote a hundred bon mots and showed that he loves bon mots.

You're open in all the right places.

The difference between paying for sex and not paying for it is that not paying for it is much more expensive.

It was so good that it felt like no harm could ever come to us.

At that moment I was released from my worldly concerns as if gliding through a starry galaxy that trailed into infinity.

It was so good that I wondered whether there would be anything left of me when we were through.

That one moment took away all others. Fear and sadness disappeared, replaced simply by joy.

He is very dedicated to his social cause. It's called Occupy Vagina.

She has a woe with wads.

It was so good that I wondered whether there would be anything left of me when we were through.

That one moment took away all others. Fear and sadness disappeared, replaced simply by joy.

MARRIAGE

My wife and I were happy for 20 years. Then we met.

Our relationship was like a tornado. There was a lot of blowing at first. Then I lost my house.

I owe my success to my first wife, and my second wife to my success.

My wife won't give me a divorce until she can find a way of doing it without making me happy.

My wife treats me like a God. She doesn't believe in me.

There are only two things necessary to keep your wife happy. First, let her think she's having her way. Second, let her have it.

My wife is a sex object. Every time I ask for sex, she objects.

He who marries for money earns every cent.

The difference between a bachelor and married man is that when a bachelor comes home, he sees what's in the refrigerator, then goes to bed. A married man comes home, sees what's in bed, then goes to the refrigerator.

A family man is someone who carries photos where is money used to be.

When two people are the most passionate and see each other in their best light, they should make an eternal commitment.

I don't see why same sex marriage is such a big deal. My wife and I have been having the same sex for over five years now.

There's a new porn magazine for married men. It has the same pictures month after month.

After my honeymoon I felt like a new man. So did my wife.

Marriage makes the highs higher and the lows more frequent.

A man is incomplete until he's married. Then he's finished.

I got married to Miss Right. I just didn't realize her first name was "Always."

Before we got married I told her I was well off. At the time I didn't realize it was true.

Since they've been married, they've been like two sides of a coin. They can't face each other, but they stay together.

There's a way to transfer funds that's even faster than electronic banking. It's called marriage.

Don't get married to make yourself happy, get married to make your spouse happy.

We've been together so long, we finish each others' threats.

Love: Temporary insanity curable by marriage.

Before I was married, I had five theories about raising children. Now I have five children and no theories.

Whether a guy ends up with a nest egg or a goose egg depends on the chick he marries.

Husbands and wives may come and go, but parents and children are forever.

If you marry a man who cheats on his wife, you will be married to a man who cheats on his wife.

Most men kiss their wives goodbye when they leave their houses. The rest kiss their houses goodbye when they leave their wives.

I never knew what real happiness was until I got married. By that time it was too late.

Marriage is a 3-ring circus: engagement ring, wedding ring, suffering.

Men have it easier. They marry later and die earlier.

Divorce: from the Latin phrase meaning to rip out a man's genitals through his wallet.

If a man opens a car door for his wife, it's either a new car or a new wife.

I got married by a judge. I should have asked for a jury.

The best husband a woman can have is an archeologist.

The older she gets, the more interested he is.

Instead of getting married, I'm going to find a girl I don't like and give her a house.

She's a good housekeeper. Every time she leaves a man, she keeps his house.

All his problems can be traced to an ancient curse known as "I now pronounce you man and wife."

Thou shalt not admit adultery.

Love is grand. Divorce is a hundred grand.

The reason divorce is so expensive is that it is worth it.

The secret of our marriage is give and take. She gives orders and I take them.

Marriage is betting half your net worth that you will love her forever, with only a 50% chance that you won't.

Love is blind. Marriage is a real eye-opener.

We used to fight because we didn't understand each other. Now we fight because we do.

I was my own worst enemy - until I got married.

She thought her marriage vows said..."for sucking all others."

My husband and I divorced over religious differences. He thought he was God and I didn't.

I have known more men destroyed by the desire to keep a wife and child in comfort than I have seen destroyed by drink and harlots.

Monogamy leaves a lot to be desired.

A bachelor is a selfish, undeserving guy who has cheated some woman out of a divorce.

A bachelor is footloose and fiance-free.

A bachelor is lucky because he can make a mistake and never know it.

We broke up for health reasons. She got sick of me.

A screwing license with steadily increasing renewal fees.

Hitler did one thing right. He killed himself immediately after getting married.

When the milk became free, I became lactose-intolerant.

When I met her, she took my breath away. Now that we're married, she just sucks the life out of me.

Hitler did one thing right. He killed himself immediately after getting married.

INTELLIGENCE

If you are the smartest person in the room, you are in the wrong room.

What she lacks in intelligence she makes up for in stupidity.

He may look like an idiot and sound like an idiot, but don't let that fool you. He IS an idiot.

A liberal arts education is not the filling of a pail; it's the lighting of a fire.

It's not the heat; it's the stupidity.

His train of thought hasn't left the station.

Ordinarily he is insane, but he has lucid moments when he is merely stupid.

He has a room temperature IQ.

When I was younger and smarter, I couldn't understand him. Now that I'm older and dumber, he makes sense to me.

He is so dense that light bends around him.

He hides his intelligence very well.

He slower than a herd of turtles stampeding through peanut butter.

He has more money than brains and he doesn't have much money.

His wit is beyond my capacity for appreciation.

He can't chew gum and think about chewing gum at the same time.

He's big enough to eat hay and dumb enough to like it.

He's so dumb, he can't even count his blessings.

The smartest thing Einstein ever did was flee Nazi Germany to save his own ass.

It is always best to attribute a quote to Einstein because no one dares contradict you.

The best way to be smart is not to do anything stupid.

He has more degrees than a thermometer.

A fool with a plan beats a genius with no plan.

He doesn't let his education get in the way of his ignorance.

Stupid? He doesn't know the meaning of the word stupid.

Great minds like a think.

Intelligence

He's not dumber than an ox, but he's not any smarter either.

Is everyone else in the world a moron? Or is it just me?

A television can insult your intelligence, but nothing rubs it in like a computer.

I'd love to screw her brains out, but it looks like someone beat me to it.

His reaction time exceeds his attention span.

My son must get his brains from his mother. I still have mine.

He is proof of reincarnation. No one can get that dumb in one lifetime.

There's a limit to my stupidity.

I've been to the circus and I've seen the elephant twice.

You can lead whore to culture, but you can't make her think.

You can lead a horse to water, but a pencil must be lead.

It was so far over my head, it didn't even mess up my hair.

Life is difficult; it's even more difficult when you're stupid.

The shortest pencil is better than the longest memory.

I'm not a complete idiot; some parts are missing.

I'm too smart to be brave.

He is unencumbered by the thought process.

I was as confused as a baby in a topless bar.

He's as sharp as a bowling ball.

He's as sharp as a wet balloon.

Dumb as a pump handle.

Dumb as a box of rocks.

Dumb as a fence post.

Artificial intelligence is no match for natural stupidity.

Perspective is worth 40 IQ points.

I may be dumb, but I'm not stupid.

Intelligence is highly overrated. It is just tricks we play with our conscious minds. Far more important, and far more rare, are integrity and honor.

He couldn't even outwit his dinner.

The more subtle, clever, and sophisticated you are, the fewer people there are who will recognize it.

He who laughs last, thinks the slowest.

The more you think, the more chance you have to be wrong.

Intelligence

Smart people make money. Very smart people read arcane books and do very difficult crossword puzzles.

He's been educated beyond his intelligence.

It ain't rocket surgery.

I'm glad I'm not as smart as he is because then I might be as wrong as he is.

I'm glad I'm not that smart because then I'd have to think a lot.

Looks

Beauty is only skin-tight.

Beauty is skin deep, but ugly is to the bone.

Beauty is only skin deep, but I'm not a cannibal.

She looks good from far away.

She is so pretty that you can't get past her face to look at her body.

She is so pretty that she will never know if she's interesting.

Being born beautiful is like being born rich and getting steadily poorer.

She has as much sex appeal as a traffic accident.

It's better to have loved and lost a short person than never to have loved a tall.

She'll rock your boxers big time.

Her legs go all the way up to her ass!

He's the triumph of sugar over diabetes.

A woman pays more attention to her looks than to her mind because many men are stupid, but few are blind.

He looks like the north end of a southbound horse.

The last time I saw a mouth like that it was about to eat Jacques Cousteau.

His good luck has not altered his standing among the physically unblessed.

He has more chins than the Hong Kong phone directory.

She has an hourglass figure; everything is gradually moving to the bottom.

She's a dark beauty. The darker it gets, the more beautiful she gets.

Every time I see her I have a fierce desire to be lonely.

When all else fails, be very good-looking.

She gets her good looks from her father; he's a plastic surgeon.

Narcissist – anyone better-looking than oneself.

Her measurements are 38-24-38, but not necessarily in that order.

I went to my reunion. My friends have become so old and fat that they couldn't recognize me.

I went to my reunion. The smart ones are still smart.

Looks

I am much bigger than my body gives me credit for.

I am not fat, I am 9 inches too short.

He's an expert at ice-boxing, well-rounded, built for comfort; not for speed.

She's so hot, she makes the ground smoke.

Hugs are better than drugs, but jugs are better than hugs.

She is so ugly, she could make a mule back away from the oatbin.

She's so ugly that dogs hump her leg with their eyes closed.

She's so ugly that when she comes into the room, the mice jump up on chairs

She's so ugly that when she was born, the doctor slapped her mother.

She's so ugly that her mother had morning sickness after she was born.

She's coyote ugly. If she falls asleep with your head on your arm, you'd rather chew your arm off than wake her up.

She's a two-bagger. One to go over her head and one to go over your head in case hers falls off.

Bald – too tall for his hair, his hair has a wide part, solar panel for sex machine.

He's not fat, he's just easy to see.

She's a real head turner alright.

She's too thick of thigh for my thinking, too stout for my snout.

Food

I'm not a vegetarian because I love animals. I am vegetarian because I hate plants.

If we weren't supposed to eat animals, why are they made of meat?

I don't eat snails; I prefer fast food.

There is no more sincere love than the love of food.

You are where you eat.

If it's made by a plant, eat it. If it's made in a plant, don't eat it.

Taste makes waist.

It would make a sword-swallower gag.

Time flies like an arrow. Fruit flies like a banana.

It is best eaten while on one's knees with one's head bare.

I couldn't possibly eat enough to vomit as much as I'd like to right now.

Within a few minutes of eating it I was driving the porcelain bus.

MONEY

It's better to be a whore than hoarder.

It's not how much is enough, it's why you feel you need more.

He's as tight as a clam's ass.

He throws quarters around like they were sewer covers.

He's so cheap, he's complimented when you call him cheap.

He's so cheap, he won't let his baby have more than one measle at a time.

He can stretch a dollar so tight that Washington weeps.

He's as tight as a rusted lug nut on a '55 Chevy.

He's so tight his shoes squeak when he walks.

He's as tight as violin strings.

He's so tight that if you shoved coal up his ass, he'd turn it into a diamond.

Broke is the new black.

Live rich, die poor.

Lay your nest egg early.

I'm a man trapped in a woman's salary.

The truth shall upset you free.

Today is the first day of the rest of your life savings.

Money is worth nothing until you spend it.

If you owe the bank $60 thousand the bank owns you.
If you owe the bank $60 million, you own the bank.

A poor person who is unhappy is in a better position than a rich person who is unhappy. He has hope. He thinks money would help.

Two pennies in piggy bank make more noise than a full one.

By the time you can make ends meet, they move the ends.

Women get minks the same way minks get minks.

The best way to treat a cold shoulder is with a mink.

He learned his lessons at the school of Fort Knox.

We're all self-made, but only the rich and successful admit it.

Money

I'd rather be rich and fat than poor and thin. You can buy your way out of fat, but you can't fat your way out of poor.

Money may not be the root of all evil, but it can sure give rise to some pretty nasty shit.

Money is the root of all technology.

The lack of money is the root of all evil.

There are two ways to be rich: 1) make more money, 2) be more selective in the things you desire.

It's better to be able to appreciate things you cannot have than to have things you cannot appreciate.

The worst things in life are free too.

Trees don't grow on money either.

The sooner you start saving money, the sooner you'll be able to borrow it.

Money can't buy happiness, but, then again, happiness can't buy money either.

Money can't buy happiness, until you give it to some-one else.

Money can't buy happiness, but it sure makes misery easier to deal with.

Money isn't everything, but it keeps you in touch with your children.

Money isn't the most important thing. Love is. It's a good thing I love money.

Money can't buy you friends, but it can sure get you a better class of enemy.

Money can't buy happiness. Give me a chance and I'll prove it to you.

Money is not important – unless you don't have it.

Love can get you through times with no money better than money can get you through times with no love.

We trade our time for money, then we trade our money for time.

They were so poor, the got married for the rice.

I'm as broke as the 10 commandments.

Living in the past has one advantage. It's cheaper.

Don't have a penny to your name? Change your name.

You can't take it with you, but you can put it where no one will ever find it.

I'm having an out-of-money experience.

Money talks. All mine ever says is goodbye.

Money is relative. The more money you have, the more relatives you have.

Money

My take home pay doesn't even get me home.

It's better to spend money like there's no tomorrow than to spend tonight like there's no money.

He has deep pockets, but short arms.

Invest in things; spend on experiences.

A penny saved is a penny you will never have to earn – ever.

A penny saved is more than a penny earned after taxes.

A man is rich in proportion to the number of things he can live without.

He has the Midas touch; everything he touches turns into a muffler.

It cost me an arm and a love handle.

Borrow money from pessimists. They don't expect it back.

Lend money to your enemies. That way, if they don't pay you, you will enjoy chasing them for it.

If you lend someone $20 and you never see them again, it was probably worth it.

The best things in life are fees.

A journey of 1,000 miles begins with a cash advance.

When my outgo exceeded my income, my upkeep was my downfall.

A fool and his money are soon spotted.

A fool and his money are soon partying.

I could retire tomorrow. But then I'd have to die next week

It's what God would have built if he had the money.

Retirement kills more people than hard work ever did.

With funds like these, who need amenities?

Waste not; whatnot.

Time is money, but money is time too. The more you spend, the less time you have. This is because money is unlimited, but time is not.

A living wage is a little bit more than you are making now.

Everyone with money to burn will meet his match.

The more money you have, the more childlike you can afford to be.

Those for whom time is money tend to substitute money for time.

He who defines his worth in purely financial terms is correct.

The Invisible Hand is on my wallet.

The only people who think about money more than rich people are poor people.

He's having his cake and eating mine too.

He bears the fruits of prosperity, without the scars of acquisition.

I know more about business than anyone who has as little money as I do.

An empty purse is heavy baggage.

Money can buy happiness if you spend it to buy more time.

I'm suffering from maltuition.

You have enough money when you can give some away.

Money doesn't change people. It just makes them more of who they already are.

You don't always get what you pay for, but you always pay for what you get.

First raise your standard of living. Then raise your standard of giving.

He reads the menu from right to left.

People who say they don't care about money are often just making an excuse not to deal with it.

INSULTS

He is a stench in the nostrils of decent people everywhere.

He's as useless as the Pope's testicles.

He's an old person's idea of what a young person is.

I don't know what your problem is, but I bet it's hard to pronounce.

You give him an inch and he thinks he's a ruler.

His crazy runs wide and deep.

He became so much nicer after he died.

His facts exceed my curiosity.

He is an unexamined life.

He's a pacifist for practical reasons - he's a coward.

She won the genetic lottery, but spent it all on clothes.

His self-awareness is not fully developed.

He's committing suicide by knife and fork.

He's trying to solve more problems than he has.

She's just as feminine as the next guy.

She's so tough, she rolls her own tampons.

His future is behind schedule.

I have the highest possible opinion of him. He's a jerk.

The best way to have a good relationship with hi is to avoid him as much as possible.

Let's make a deal. You don't criticize what I'm eating and I won't criticize your personality.

You're in pretty good shape for the shape you're in.

What are you going to do for a face when the baboon wants his ass back?

He sits on the sidelines uttering snide lines.

Her problem is that she lacks the power of conversation, but not the power of speech.

He regards free speech not so much as a right as a continuing obligation.

He should try out for goalie on the darts team.

His purpose in life is to serve as a warning to others.

He has an inferiority complex, but not a very good one.

The more I think of him, the less I think of him.

Instead of being born again, he should just grow up.

I like your approach. Now let's see your departure.

There's no beginning to his talents.

That shirt puts the U in ugly.

I have no respect for him because he does not try to get the things that he wants.

He must have been born upside down. His nose runs and his feet smell.

He was the last one in his family to go to college. He's an evolutionary dead end.

The fact that no one understands you does not mean you're an artist.

He's so narrow-minded he can see through a keyhole with both eyes.

He is so narrow-minded you could use his brain to slice salami.

He is so narrow-minded he has to stack his prejudices vertically.

I've been called worse by better men.

He has an edifice complex.

He is the illegitimate spawn of a rogue and a harlot.

She's a bag of loose nuts and bolts.

He's trying to walk in his father's footsteps with feet half his father's size.

He has a mind like a steel trap; rusty and illegal in 37 states.

He's memorized the words, but he hasn't quite got the tune.

Imitation is the sincerest form of flattery, but mocking is the sincerest form of insult.

He's lower than whale shit.

Behind his smile is a set of sharp teeth.

He's a yellow-bellied, androgen-deprived, hypo-gonadal girlie-man.

Get up on your hind legs and think about it.

You are wise beyond your height.

He's so short that when it rains, he's the last to know.

He is Dale Carnegie's evil twin – nasty, brutish, and short.

He's all hat, no cattle. All boots, no saddle.

He's all dick, no balls.

She's all trash, no trailer.

Insults

She leaves little to the imagination, but lots to be desired.

That idea is about as good as something between going behind your boss's back and calling your ex at 2:00 in the morning while drunk.

He measures his generosity by the amount of advice he gives.

If I didn't like you so much, I think I'd insult you right now.

A nice ass should be seen, not heard.

He's as rudderless as a jellyfish.

He has an amazing ability for stating the obvious.

Take him out of my misery.

He fits in like a cat in a dog pound.

If I agreed with you, we'd both be wrong.

If you stop telling lies about me, I'll stop telling the truth about you.

I'd treat you like an equal, but I'm afraid you'd do the same for me.

She look like she been rode hard and put away wet.

He's progressed from festering lesion to oozing pustule.

His opinions exceed his experience.

His words exceed his influence.

He's mountain climbing over molehills.

He's majoring in minor things.

He put first things first, but never got past first. He's in the thick of thin things.

If humans are God's language, you're an obscenity.

He doesn't open his mouth without subtracting from the sum of human knowledge.

He's a sheep in sheep's clothing.

He has a wishbone where his backbone should be.

He's having an out-of-mind experience.

When she leaves the room, the lights get brighter.

He speaks with a certainty so far greater than his knowledge that you wonder if he even believes what he says.

She's a weepy, estrogen-bloated, mass of conflicting emotions.

He can compress the most words into the smallest idea of anyone I know.

I've seen wounds that were better dressed.

He was born under the sign of the bull.

He chews more than he bites off.

Before they made him they broke the mold.

I upped my standards. Up yours.

He breathes my oxygen when he's in the room.

He's the salt of the earth...and I'm an open wound.

He is firmly in the grip of his own compulsions.

He's often wrong, but never in doubt.

He was born on third base and thought he hit a triple.

He was born with a silver foot in his mouth.

He's the pushiest person since Sisyphus.

I'm looking for someone a little closer to the top of the food chain.

I have my father's pride and my mother's contempt for my father.

I went to his funeral just to make sure he was dead.

I wouldn't say he's a doormat; he's not that valuable.

There's nothing wrong with him that reincarnation won't cure.

He loves nature, despite what it did to him.

Some people cause happiness wherever the go. He causes happiness whenever he goes.

He has delusions of gender.

His smell could knock a buzzard off a shitwagon.

He has as much chance as a fart in a windstorm.

He was waiting with open asshole.

He pisses in the darkest corners of my soul.

He believes life is not fair and is constantly trying to prove it.

He's as empty as a jar of peanut butter in the trash.

He's a waste of carbon.

He's watching a movie only he can see.

Despite his lack of self-esteem, he consistently underestimates himself.

He is ashamed of his group, so he only identifies with it for purposes of being offended.

The only thing more insulting to a woman than telling her she'd make a good receptacle is to tell her she wouldn't make a good one.

He's a disengaged and heavy spirit.

His need to prove himself right is so strong that he fails to recognize that people despise him for it.

His problem is that, wherever he goes, he's there.

You have to know him really well to dislike him.

His desire to do the right thing is a great deal stronger than his ability to discern just what the right thing might be.

He created his own reality, but then he forgot what he did.

He's a wandering generality.

What he lacks in testicular volume, he makes up for in politeness.

He seems to have no ability to observe himself.

He's as ambitious as Lucifer.

If it weren't for his double standards, he would have no standards at all.

She's a menopausal, non-orgasmic, penis-envying jezebel.

He's not like stopped clock that is right twice a day. He is more like a slow clock that is hardly ever right.

I agree that I should embrace my mistakes, but you smell really bad right now.

He's like a slinky – not really good for anything, but you can't help but smile when you see him tumbling down the stairs.

He's a connoisseur of his own neurosis.

When she was walking away she looked like two bulldogs fighting inside a burlap sack.

He's not fat, he's just very easy to see.

He's trying to scrimp his way to prosperity.

Joy is a thing he experiences only by stealing it from others.

You ain't worth the busted rubber that got you born.

Your mother made two mistakes. The second was not abandoning you for the jackels to devour.

His nose is so big because the air is free.

If he were drowning, I would throw him a life preserver, but I wouldn't feel bad if he didn't get it.

He reads he bible, but just to look for loopholes.

She went to school of hard knockers.

He can pass time more effectively than anyone I've ever known.

If I weren't so dumb, I wouldn't like you so much.

He wants to move to a country where farting is considered a compliment to the host.

He thinks deeply about life, but hasn't come up with anything except ordinary thoughts.

He has the body of a Greek diner.

He has done a really good job of finding out what doesn't work.

She's a rancid bag of expired meat.

METAPHORS & SIMILES

As thin as turnip soup.

As lean as a lizzard.

Complacent as a cow.

It was forged with the hot steel of raw courage.

He's as straight as six o'clock.

He's putting Descartes before Horace.

It's as easy as opening a can of peas with your fingers.

As right as waking up in the morning.

It's like hot soup on a cold day.

Toilet oysters.

It was like trying to sew a button on custard pie.

That thought is so deep you need a diving bell to understand it.

The earth laughs in flowers.

It blew me away like a tornado through a trailer park.

He was as blunt as a butcher.

She looked at me as if I were a side dish she hadn't ordered.

He was the skunk at the garden party.

Music is what feelings sound like.

Tears are words the heart can't express.

As nervous as a cat.

As independent as a hog on ice.

Calm as a lizard on a rock.

Smug as a fat house cat.

As free as the wind on an open plain.

It's as uncouth as asking a deaf person to be quiet.

It was a tough as a $3 steak.

It loomed like Banquo's ghost.

He is cold as yesterday's mashed potatoes.

It was colder than a nun's pussy on Sunday.

It was like trying to launch the invasion of Normandy.

It sounded like Patton taking Belgium.

As fragile as a soap bubble.

It was as snug as a sausage casing.

It's like digging in granite.

That was closer than the pages in a book.

Make water, shake the snake, let the monster out to feed the flowers, have a liquidity event

Arm job (hug).

As welcome as the flowers in May.

He was passing gas like a NASCAR pit crew.

I absorbed it from the breast milk of my mother.

A plume of doubt that hung in the air like cigar smoke.

I'd be all over that like it was the last chopper out of 'Nam.

I'd be all over that like hair on soap.

I'd be all over that like a bum on a ham sandwich.

I'm on that like a numerator on a denominator.

The forgiving cloak of night.

As nervous as a pig in a packing plant.

I'd bet on him in a butt-kicking contest even if he had just one leg.

That follows like a shadow.

It's like gargling with peanut butter.

The early worm gets caught.

The early bird may get the worm, but the second mouse gets the cheese.

The early fish gets hooked by the same thing that the early bird gets credit for.

The answers appeared like candy wrappers the day after Halloween.

I curse the mother of the man who cut the tree that made the paper that that bon mot was written on.

The spouting whale gets the harpoon.

As sudden as a broken shoelace.

As natural as water running down a hill.

My tears have reached the sea and I am ready to move on.

It snuck up on me like wolves on cattle.

Time sneaks up on you like a windshield on a bug.

It settled on me like a gentle snow.

The patience of a stump.

It's like trying to French kiss through a screen door.

The finer the net is woven, the more numerous the holes.

A nest of vipers.

A cauldron of woes.

It vanished like a magician's assistant in a box.

He gave the one-figured salute.

He displayed his driving finger.

Uncategorizable

Women's intuition is the result of millions of years of not thinking.

I may not be able to explain it, or even understand it, but my being correct does not depend on my being able to explain or understand it.

I'm not afraid of heights; I'm afraid of widths.

We've all heard that a million monkeys banging on a million typewriters will eventually produce the complete works of Shakespeare. Now, thanks to the Internet, we know this is not true.

The art of conversation is not only to say the right thing at the right time, but to leave unsaid the wrong thing at the tempting moment.

I did not slap him. I high-fived his face, I applauded him with one hand.

Music is the silence between the notes.

Give me a set of golf clubs, green grass, a sunny day, and a beautiful companion and you can keep the golf clubs.

Running late does not count as exercise.

A picture is worth a thousand words, but it uses up 3,000 times more memory.

A pinch of probability is worth a pound of perhaps.

As long as you are going to feel guilty, you might as well be guilty of something.

There are some things about which nothing can be said.

I want quality, not quantity, but lots of it.

A man's house is his hassle.

Religion is man's quest for assurance that he won't be dead when he will be.

A good pun is its own reword.

I made ten puns in the hope that one would make him laugh. But no pun in ten did.

They laughed when I told them I was writing a book of puns. Well, they're not laughing now.

A Freudian slip is when you say one thing, but mean your mother.

I don't love New York, I just hate everywhere else.

Technology is a way of ordering the universe so that people don't have to experience it.

Thanks for the book. I'll waste no time reading it.

What was the best thing before sliced bread?

It's the best thing since the birth control pill.

You'll dig yourself into a hole so deep that people won't know where you're buried.

A person is not really dead until the last person who knew him dies.

We'll burn that bridge when we come to it.

I do whatever my Rice Krispies tell me to.

Well, I'm here. What are your other two wishes?

Is the glass half full? Yes, half full of air.

Is the glass half full? Yes, and half full of water, because glasses were made to hold water, not air.

The glass isn't half full, it's twice as big as it needs to be.

Whether the glass is half full or half empty depends on whether you're pouring or drinking.

After a certain age the glass is half full because you need somewhere to keep your teeth.

The glass is half full with water. The rest is hot air from you.

My gun has a point and click interface.

Suicide is the sincerest form of self-criticism.

I know you believe you understood what you think I said, but I'm not sure you realize that what you heard is not what I meant.

There is logic to my actions. I just need to figure out what it is.

A witty saying proves nothing.

I dream of one day living in a world where a chicken can cross the street without having its motives questioned.

GOODBYE

Carry on.

Happy trails.

Keep on truckin'.

It's been emotional.

Ye shall be as a god!

May the gods guide you gently my friend!

Keep it out of the ditch.

Keep the greasy side down.

Peace, brother.

You're in charge.

Hang on tight!

I hope you get what you deserve.

Cheerio!

Sweet dreams my friend.

Keep the faith!

Party on, dude!

Bye Bye Bye.

It's been real, and it's been fun, but it hasn't been real fun.

May your spawn flourish.

Good-bye and Good Luck!

Stay alive!

Keep a cool stool.

Bonus

Revealed: The Meaning of Life

Grasshopper: What is the meaning of life?

Master: If you want to know the meaning of life, look up "life" in the dictionary. If you are not satisfied with that answer, there must be something is wrong with your question.

Grasshopper: No, this is a very important question that needs to be answered!

Master: Your question assumes that life has some special kind of meaning, other than the kind of meaning that everything else has. But why does life have to have such a meaning? What is the meaning of a chair, other than to sit in it? What is the meaning of life other than how we should live it? It seems there is a problem with your use of the word "meaning."

It seems that what you really want to know is not the meaning of life, but something else, like what the purpose of your life is. If you ask the purpose of your life, the question makes more sense, but still needs clarification. The purpose of something is what the best use of it is.

Looked at in this way, the question can now be answered. For many, the purpose of their lives is to enjoy it, to become as fully as they can who they are as their unique selves, and to then to die. As part of this, you can also strive to contribute to the common good by helping others enjoy their own lives and fulfill their own genetic potential, but you could also simply strive to more fully experience your relationship with the universe. By doing this, you do your part in helping the universe unfold.

So your problem is not that life has no meaning, but that you feel it should have meaning. A life without a more directed and preordained meaning frees us from dogma and the expectations of others and it can be liberating. You don't have to believe some greater force is leading you in a specific direction in order to know you're going in the right direction.

The parable of the kitten and cat is useful on this point. The kitten is chasing his tail around and around. The cat asks the kitten why he is chasing his tail. The kitten replies that he has heard that the secret of happiness is in the tail. The cat replies that, "You are right that the secret of life is in the tail. However, I've found that, if I just go about my business, happiness just follows me around wherever I go."

Grasshopper: Ok, smart guy, but I'm still not satisfied. What I really want to know is Where did I come from?

What caused me to be here?

Master: If the purpose of life is simply to live, it doesn't matter where we came from, or by what force. It is not productive to continue to ask a question for which you will not find an answer. In any case, no longer needing to ask a question can be as good as getting the answer. What if you found out that humans were planted on earth for consumption by the residents of planet Xircon? Wouldn't you rather not know that and to just live your life?

If you are comforted by believing in fairy tales, go ahead! Living this way does not require religious belief; it is religious experience. Just don't let it detract from your living fully. If you figure out where we came from, please let me know. In the meantime, I'm going to eat something.

Grasshopper: So what happens to us when we die?

Master: You didn't come into this world, you came out of, like a wave from an ocean. And so you will you go back into it. What you think of as your individual self will dissolve and merge back into the infinite mix of everything that you came from. You lose your ego completely. What could be more comforting than that?

Grasshopper: I just don't see how it all could have started. I always get back to how all this can come from nothing, like which came first: the chick or the egg?

Master: Oh, that one is easy! The chicken had to come first because a chicken can survive without an egg, but an egg can't survive without a chicken! You will not be satisfied with that answer either and for the same reason – because you are not asking your real question.

I'm tired of all this. Perhaps you can find satisfaction in the answer to one of the greatest questions of all time: Why don't men ask for directions? They don't ask for directions because they don't feel lost! All who wander are not lost! The journey is the challenge. Better to accept the challenge and enjoy it on its various levels than to fret.

Grasshopper: So that's it? Just stop asking questions?

Master: Close, but you just asked two more questions.

* * *

Still reading?!

Here's Bonus #2:

How to Win an Argument

While Being Wrong

We all would like to be able to convince others that we are right. Much has been written on how to persuade people and how to win an argument. However, such advice assumes that what you are saying is actually true! What if you are wrong and your pride won't let you admit it? What if you could deflect all criticism, appear correct, and feel good about it?

Such things are possible. What follows are not cheap tricks like personal attacks on the arguer. They are conversation-stoppers that are far more effective. However, first you must admit to yourself that you are wrong, unwilling to admit to others that you are wrong, and can't win with facts or logic.

We all know the old standbys of answering a question with a question, changing the subject, and just ignoring someone.

But these are not always possible. So here are a few ways to deflect attention from your inability to prevail on the merits.

Suppose you have done something in a public place that opened you us to a criticism from a passerby. Rather than try to explain or excuse your behavior, you have a very good chance of deflecting the criticism by asking, "Who are you?"

It is such a common, and expected, courtesy for a person to identify themselves before speaking substantively to a stranger, that this can provide a good escape route if you can follow up with similar questions or further techniques.

For example, a great all-purpose follow up question is, "Why do you ask?" This deflects the subject and forces your inquisitor to justify his nosiness, which there is a good chance he will not attempt to do. This question is so powerful that it will cause many inquisitors to simply throw their hands up and say, "Forget it!"

If that doesn't work, try "How does that make you feel?" The angry reaction to that may be something like "How does it make me feel? What does that have to do with anything?" The trap shuts. You reply, "Well, of all the possible things you could have focused on and thought about, you mentioned that. Therefore, you must have had a strong emotional reaction. So I ask you again, how does that make you feel?" If your poor challenger has not yet slinked away muttering, he is probably thoroughly disarmed.

Whatever your misdeeds or poor behavior, if you've practiced not blinking or blushing when you are caught, you are way ahead. Imagine getting caught beforehand and practicing response so you aren't surprised. Then subtly shift the blame to your challenger. You might say, "It's ok that you feel that way. There's nothing wrong with that." Ha! That's so condescending that it's bound to shift the emotional weight of the exchange. You may appear boorish, but you will not appear wrong! If he relates his own personal experiences you can ask, "Does it help?" or "Is that important to you?" and effectively turn the conversation to his being the one with the problem.

In the same vein, an all-purpose reaction, when you can't think of something else, is a loud "Wow!" It immediately makes your now-shaky foe wonder what he said that was so wrong.

After patiently listening to your new friend's well-argued criticism of your behavior, you can also respond simply, "So what's your point?" This will leave most people exasperated.

If he confronts you with facts that you are unable to challenge, you can always simply say, "I don't believe it." Whatever the facts are, whatever the study says, you don't have to believe it! Declaring that you just don't believe it leaves your factual friend with little room to dump further information on you. If he challenges your position and asks for an example, you can just say, "I don't need to have an example in order to be right."

Perhaps by now your once-proud challenger is himself looking for a dignified way out. Give it to him. You might flatly say "I'm not going to argue about that." What a concept! No one can force the direction of a conversation on you. At the risk of really setting him off, you could deliver some variation on "I'm sorry. I don't want to embarrass you" or "I can explain it for you, but I can't comprehend it for you" or "Your comment is not helpful."

Want more? Memorize some general, but difficult to grasp quote from Aristotle. Quoting Aristotle has the strange effect of leaving people wide-eyed and slack-jawed. Another favorite is to say, "If I did that, it would like Dioneses appearing at the gates of Thebes." It is very unlikely anyone is going to know what the hell you are talking about and they won't want to reveal their ignorance.

Still, you may have run into a sharpie and have to defend your poor arguments with something that more closely resembles truth. In that case, consider the following:

Did he contradict your argument with facts? "That's the exception that proves the rule."

Did he ask you if you did something wrong? "If I did, I certainly wouldn't admit it."

Did he ask you some other question you can't answer? You could just ignore him, but you could probably make it more fun. Take the lead from politicians. How about, "I'm glad you asked that question, I'm sorry what's your name? Bob, ok, Bob, I 'm glad you asked that question, Bob" and then go on to make some completely unrelated point. How about "The real question is ____ (and then go on and on). If he interrupts, say, "I let you finish your point, now let me finish mine. You've been dominating the conversation. Now it's my turn." Then just keep talking.

Need a few more ways to exasperate your new pal? How about, "I don't have to be consistent because I'm not trying to convince you of anything." Or "Take a deep breath and focus."

Are you getting desperate? Spill a drink or cause some other distraction. How about, "No Eenglesh" or "Ees tradeeshun in my cone-tree." (In that case, it's alright!)

And the best, last, all-purpose line you have, with a big grin and lots of eye contact, ask "Crazy world, ain't it?"

After all this, you have now established a bond with your worthy adversary. Introduce yourself, shake his hand, offer to buy him a cup of coffee so you can talk more. Don't worry; he won't accept.

* * *